About Skill Builders
Math
Grade 5

Welcome to Skill Builders *Math* for fifth grade. This book is designed to improve children's math skills through focused practice.

This full-color workbook contains grade-level-appropriate activities based on national standards to help ensure that children master basic skills before progressing.

More than 70 pages of activities cover essential math skills, such as multiplication and division, fractions, geometry, and data analysis. The book's colorful, inviting format, easy-to-follow directions, and clear examples help build children's confidence and make math more accessible and enjoyable.

The Skill Builders series offers workbooks that are perfect for keeping skills sharp during the school year or preparing students for the next grade.

Credits:
Content Editor: JulieAnna Kirsch
Copy Editor: Beatrice Allen
Layout and Cover Design: Nick Greenwood

www.carsondellosa.com
Carson-Dellosa Publishing LLC
Greensboro, North Carolina

ISBN 978-1-936023-27-1
03-156121151

Table of Contents

Rounding Whole Numbers

The chart shows the land and water area of different states. Complete the chart by rounding each state's area to the nearest thousand and hundred.

State	Area in Square Miles	Rounded to Nearest Thousands	Rounded to Nearest Hundreds
Alabama	52,419	**52,000**	**52,400**
1. Alaska	663,267		
2. California	163,696		
3. Delaware	2,489		
4. Georgia	59,425		
5. Kansas	82,277		
6. Maryland	12,407		
7. Mississippi	48,430		
8. Nevada	110,561		
9. New York	54,556		
10. Oregon	98,381		
11. Rhode Island	1,545		
12. Texas	268,581		
13. Wyoming	97,814		
14. Colorado	104,094		
15. Kansas	82,277		
16. Maine	35,385		
17. New Mexico	121,589		
18. North Carolina	53,819		
19. Vermont	9,614		
20. Idaho	83,570		

Place Value

Write each number in standard form.

1. 50,000 + 2,000 + 500 + 70 + 6 _____

2. 20,000 + 6,000 + 900 + 10 + 5 _____

3. 430,000 + 4,000 + 600 + 20 + 9 _____

4. 960,000 + 8,000 + 300 + 30 + 1 _____

5. 640,000 + 20,000 + 100 + 80 + 2 _____

6. 850,000 + 80,000 + 3,000 + 500 + 7 _____

7. 450,000 + 7,000 + 200 + 20 + 9 _____

8. 200,000 + 3,000 + 800 + 70 + 4 _____

Write each number in expanded form.

9. 46,279 _____

10. 60,542 _____

11. 378,720 _____

12. 112,305 _____

Place Value

Write each number in standard form.

1. 2 ten thousands, 7 hundreds, 3 tens, and 1 one

   _____

2. 3 ten thousands, 4 thousands, 7 hundreds, 3 tens, and 0 ones

   _____

3. 6 ten thousands, 2 hundreds, 7 tens, and 3 ones

   _____

4. 2 ten thousands, 7 thousands, 6 hundreds, 9 tens, and 4 ones

   _____

5. 1 ten thousand, 6 thousands, 7 hundreds, 9 tens, and 2 ones

   _____

6. 8 ten thousands, 9 thousands, 4 hundreds, 6 tens, and 3 ones

   _____

7. 3 ten thousands, 6 thousands, 8 hundreds, 3 tens, and 5 ones

   _____

8. 2 hundred thousands, 3 ten thousands, 5 hundreds, 8 tens, and 9 ones

   _____

9. 2 millions, 6 hundred thousands, 7 ten thousands, 4 hundreds, 9 ones

   _____

Comparing Numbers

Compare each pair of numbers. Use >, <, or =.

17,021 (<) 17,210   1. 643 ( ) 463

2. 632,972 ( ) 623,792   3. 41,101 ( ) 41,001

4. 864,916 ( ) 864,619   5. 34,400 ( ) 34,400

6. 6,729 ( ) 6,927   7. 454,680 ( ) 454,086

8. 101,000 ( ) 110,000   9. 909,464 ( ) 909,644

10. 31,001 ( ) 31,101   11. 7,579 ( ) 7,579

12. 879,301 ( ) 879,031   13. 85,101 ( ) 85,001

14. 609,766 ( ) 609,676   15. 407,101 ( ) 409,101

16. 1,394,201 ( ) 1,394,201   17. 2,129,753 ( ) 2,129,573

Estimating

Round each item to the nearest dollar. Use the rounded prices to estimate the amount of each shopping list.

bananas, 2 bags of sugar, and cereal
$1.00 + $2.00 + $2.00 + $4.00 = $9.00

1. 3 loaves of bread, milk, and eggs

2. eggs, flour, and cheese

3. bananas and 3 packages of cereal

4. 2 cartons of eggs, cheese, and bananas

5. sugar, 2 cartons of milk, and cheese

Addition with Regrouping

Solve each problem.

```
  1 1
  176        1.    945      2.   4,855     3.   9,423
+ 549           + 754          + 6,806        + 3,750
─────
  725
```

4. 36,761   5. 79,246   6. 43,751   7. 85,243
  + 74,485   + 51,184   + 67,169   + 13,267

8.   464   9.   161   10.   468   11.   991
      653   363   616   597
    + 444   + 186   + 787   + 227

12. 6,254   13. 8,644   14. 7,423   15. 6,064
     5,401   2,645   8,531   4,008
     4,674   2,752   1,754   7,640
   + 3,125   + 1,660   + 4,405   + 1,028

Addition with Regrouping

Solve each problem.

$$\begin{array}{r} {\scriptstyle 1} \\ 5{,}136 \\ + 2{,}549 \\ \hline \mathbf{7{,}685} \end{array}$$

1.
$$\begin{array}{r} 3{,}453 \\ + 7{,}465 \\ \hline \end{array}$$

2.
$$\begin{array}{r} 74{,}531 \\ + 30{,}593 \\ \hline \end{array}$$

3.
$$\begin{array}{r} 15{,}472 \\ + 40{,}765 \\ \hline \end{array}$$

4.
$$\begin{array}{r} 915{,}341 \\ + 65{,}433 \\ \hline \end{array}$$

5.
$$\begin{array}{r} 103{,}256 \\ + 67{,}525 \\ \hline \end{array}$$

6.
$$\begin{array}{r} 545{,}971 \\ + 31{,}716 \\ \hline \end{array}$$

7.
$$\begin{array}{r} 673{,}665 \\ + 41{,}698 \\ \hline \end{array}$$

8.
$$\begin{array}{r} 435{,}467 \\ + 674{,}577 \\ \hline \end{array}$$

9.
$$\begin{array}{r} 933{,}845 \\ + 127{,}747 \\ \hline \end{array}$$

10.
$$\begin{array}{r} 893{,}863 \\ + 953{,}523 \\ \hline \end{array}$$

11.
$$\begin{array}{r} 456{,}768 \\ + 854{,}127 \\ \hline \end{array}$$

12.
$$\begin{array}{r} 5{,}656 \\ 8{,}656 \\ 3{,}642 \\ + 1{,}599 \\ \hline \end{array}$$

13.
$$\begin{array}{r} 9{,}003 \\ 5{,}855 \\ 9{,}673 \\ + 3{,}794 \\ \hline \end{array}$$

14.
$$\begin{array}{r} 5{,}567 \\ 1{,}355 \\ 2{,}078 \\ + 5{,}853 \\ \hline \end{array}$$

15.
$$\begin{array}{r} 6{,}742 \\ 2{,}153 \\ 9{,}432 \\ + 4{,}117 \\ \hline \end{array}$$

Subtraction with Regrouping

Solve each problem.

```
        12
     4 1⅔ 12
       5̶3̶2̶        1.    648      2.    354      3.    674
     – 165            – 497           – 285           – 158
       367
```

4.   854   5.   773   6.   544   7.   634
    – 169   – 487   – 375   – 479

8.   4,551   9.   7,452   10.   1,531   11.   8,451
    – 2,957   – 3,284   – 1,368   – 4,276

12.   7,681   13.   3,002   14.   7,515   15.   9,461
    – 5,099   – 1,698   – 2,907   – 2,576

Subtraction with Regrouping

Solve each problem.

$$\begin{array}{r} \overset{17}{\underset{}{\cancel{8}}}\overset{}{\cancel{9}}\overset{14}{\cancel{4}} \\ 1,\cancel{9}\cancel{8}\cancel{4} \\ -\ \ \ 487 \\ \hline 1,497 \end{array}$$

1. $\begin{array}{r} 4,435 \\ -\ \ 579 \\ \hline \end{array}$

2. $\begin{array}{r} 7,381 \\ -\ 1,979 \\ \hline \end{array}$

3. $\begin{array}{r} 6,674 \\ -\ 2,767 \\ \hline \end{array}$

4. $\begin{array}{r} 5,374 \\ -\ \ 887 \\ \hline \end{array}$

5. $\begin{array}{r} 9,757 \\ -\ 3,569 \\ \hline \end{array}$

6. $\begin{array}{r} 2,673 \\ -\ 2,194 \\ \hline \end{array}$

7. $\begin{array}{r} 3,734 \\ -\ 2,755 \\ \hline \end{array}$

8. $\begin{array}{r} 24,762 \\ -\ 6,268 \\ \hline \end{array}$

9. $\begin{array}{r} 43,642 \\ -\ 8,286 \\ \hline \end{array}$

10. $\begin{array}{r} 39,003 \\ -\ 4,357 \\ \hline \end{array}$

11. $\begin{array}{r} 17,041 \\ -\ 2,353 \\ \hline \end{array}$

12. $\begin{array}{r} 64,546 \\ -\ 8,349 \\ \hline \end{array}$

13. $\begin{array}{r} 90,442 \\ -\ 6,346 \\ \hline \end{array}$

14. $\begin{array}{r} 15,753 \\ -\ 2,657 \\ \hline \end{array}$

15. $\begin{array}{r} 75,604 \\ -\ 23,892 \\ \hline \end{array}$

Multiplication and Division Facts

Complete each multiplication or division fact.

1. $6 \times 9 =$ _____

2. $15 \div 3 =$ _____

3. $36 \div 4 =$ _____

4. $6 \times 4 =$ _____

5. $16 \div$ _____ $= 4$

6. $30 \div 5 =$ _____

7. _____ $\div 6 = 5$

8. $18 \div$ _____ $= 3$

9. $24 \div$ _____ $= 2$

10. _____ $\div 8 = 6$

11. _____ $\div 9 = 7$

12. $20 \div$ _____ $= 2$

13. $49 \div 7 =$ _____

14. _____ $\div 2 = 6$

15. $144 \div 12 =$ _____

16. $84 \div 7 =$ _____

17. $21 \div$ _____ $= 3$

18. $14 \div 2 =$ _____

19. $72 \div 9 =$ _____

20. $6 \div 3 =$ _____

21. _____ $\times 4 = 20$

22. _____ $\times 8 = 24$

23. $5 \times$ _____ $= 25$

24. $9 \times$ _____ $= 81$

25. $44 \div 11 =$ _____

26. $40 \div 5 =$ _____

27. _____ $\times 9 = 81$

28. _____ $\times 8 = 88$

29. $8 \times$ _____ $= 32$

30. $45 \div 9 =$ _____

31. $7 \times$ _____ $= 28$

32. _____ $\times 8 = 64$

Multiplying Multiples of 10

Solve each problem.

	If...	Then...
	12	12
	× 3	× 30
	36	**360**

1. 53
    × 10

2. 12
    × 20

3. 43
    × 30

4. 26
    × 40

5. 42
    × 50

6. 25
    × 20

7. 39
    × 20

8. 16
    × 30

9. 35
    × 10

10. 36
    × 30

11. 44
    × 40

12. 23
    × 50

13. 625
    × 30

14. 318
    × 40

15. 194
    × 20

16. 216
    × 40

Multiplication with Regrouping

Solve each problem.

$$\begin{array}{r} ^2 64 \\ \times\ 7 \\ \hline \mathbf{448} \end{array}$$

1.
$$\begin{array}{r} 87 \\ \times\ 20 \\ \hline \end{array}$$

2.
$$\begin{array}{r} 17 \\ \times\ 6 \\ \hline \end{array}$$

3.
$$\begin{array}{r} 92 \\ \times\ 5 \\ \hline \end{array}$$

4.
$$\begin{array}{r} 771 \\ \times\ 2 \\ \hline \end{array}$$

5.
$$\begin{array}{r} 365 \\ \times\ 6 \\ \hline \end{array}$$

6.
$$\begin{array}{r} 204 \\ \times\ 3 \\ \hline \end{array}$$

7.
$$\begin{array}{r} 880 \\ \times\ 7 \\ \hline \end{array}$$

8.
$$\begin{array}{r} 414 \\ \times\ 7 \\ \hline \end{array}$$

9.
$$\begin{array}{r} 189 \\ \times\ 4 \\ \hline \end{array}$$

10.
$$\begin{array}{r} 507 \\ \times\ 5 \\ \hline \end{array}$$

11.
$$\begin{array}{r} 248 \\ \times\ 6 \\ \hline \end{array}$$

12.
$$\begin{array}{r} 6,479 \\ \times\ 9 \\ \hline \end{array}$$

13.
$$\begin{array}{r} 5,478 \\ \times\ 814 \\ \hline \end{array}$$

14.
$$\begin{array}{r} 1,367 \\ \times\ 4 \\ \hline \end{array}$$

15.
$$\begin{array}{r} 2,247 \\ \times\ 3 \\ \hline \end{array}$$

Multiplication with Regrouping

Solve each problem.

Multiply by the ones digit.

$$\overset{2}{2}9$$
$$\times\ 23$$
$$29 \times 3 \longrightarrow 87$$

Multiply by the tens digit.

$$\overset{1}{\overset{2}{2}}9$$
$$\times\ 23$$
$$\overline{87}$$
$$29 \times 20 \longrightarrow 580$$

Placeholder ↑

Add the partial products.

$$\overset{1}{\overset{2}{2}}9$$
$$\times\ 23$$
$$\overline{87}$$
$$+\ 580$$
$$\overline{667}$$

1.
$$\begin{array}{r} 87 \\ \times\ 41 \\ \hline \end{array}$$

2.
$$\begin{array}{r} 58 \\ \times\ 27 \\ \hline \end{array}$$

3.
$$\begin{array}{r} 45 \\ \times\ 16 \\ \hline \end{array}$$

4.
$$\begin{array}{r} 90 \\ \times\ 23 \\ \hline \end{array}$$

5.
$$\begin{array}{r} 71 \\ \times\ 22 \\ \hline \end{array}$$

6.
$$\begin{array}{r} 85 \\ \times\ 86 \\ \hline \end{array}$$

7.
$$\begin{array}{r} 17 \\ \times\ 53 \\ \hline \end{array}$$

8.
$$\begin{array}{r} 37 \\ \times\ 97 \\ \hline \end{array}$$

9.
$$\begin{array}{r} 26 \\ \times\ 49 \\ \hline \end{array}$$

10.
$$\begin{array}{r} 34 \\ \times\ 76 \\ \hline \end{array}$$

11.
$$\begin{array}{r} 65 \\ \times\ 25 \\ \hline \end{array}$$

12.
$$\begin{array}{r} 18 \\ \times\ 24 \\ \hline \end{array}$$

Multiplication with Regrouping

Solve each problem.

$$\begin{array}{r} \overset{1\ 1}{\underset{}{}} \\ \overset{7\ 6}{\underset{}{}} \\ 487 \\ \times\ 29 \\ \hline 4{,}383 \\ +\ 9{,}740 \\ \hline \mathbf{14{,}123} \end{array}$$

1.
$$\begin{array}{r} 471 \\ \times\ 23 \\ \hline \end{array}$$

2.
$$\begin{array}{r} 268 \\ \times\ 40 \\ \hline \end{array}$$

3.
$$\begin{array}{r} 372 \\ \times\ 24 \\ \hline \end{array}$$

4.
$$\begin{array}{r} 397 \\ \times\ 46 \\ \hline \end{array}$$

5.
$$\begin{array}{r} 140 \\ \times\ 37 \\ \hline \end{array}$$

6.
$$\begin{array}{r} 297 \\ \times\ 80 \\ \hline \end{array}$$

7.
$$\begin{array}{r} 117 \\ \times\ 68 \\ \hline \end{array}$$

8.
$$\begin{array}{r} 537 \\ \times\ 26 \\ \hline \end{array}$$

9.
$$\begin{array}{r} 117 \\ \times\ 79 \\ \hline \end{array}$$

10.
$$\begin{array}{r} 976 \\ \times\ 26 \\ \hline \end{array}$$

11.
$$\begin{array}{r} 347 \\ \times\ 53 \\ \hline \end{array}$$

12.
$$\begin{array}{r} 447 \\ \times\ 47 \\ \hline \end{array}$$

13.
$$\begin{array}{r} 540 \\ \times\ 55 \\ \hline \end{array}$$

14.
$$\begin{array}{r} 138 \\ \times\ 95 \\ \hline \end{array}$$

15.
$$\begin{array}{r} 294 \\ \times\ 59 \\ \hline \end{array}$$

Division without Remainders

Solve each problem.

3)78

Step 1: What number times 3 is closest to, but less than or equal to, 7?

3 × 1 = 3 too small
3 × **2** = 6
3 × 3 = 9 too big

Step 2: Write 2 above the tens column. Write the product of 3 × 2 under the tens column. Subtract and bring down the 8 from the ones column.

$$\begin{array}{r} 2 \\ 3\overline{)78} \\ -6\!\downarrow \\ \hline 18 \end{array}$$

Step 3: What number times 3 is closest to, but less than or equal to, 18?

3 × 6 = 18

$$\begin{array}{r} 26 \\ 3\overline{)78} \\ -6 \\ \hline 18 \\ -18 \\ \hline 0 \end{array}$$

1. 3)57

2. 7)182

3. 8)336

4. 6)558

5. 2)98

6. 5)140

7. 3)252

8. 4)268

9. 5)325

Division with Remainders

Solve each problem.

$9\overline{)782}$

What number times 9 is closest to, but less than or equal to, 782? (Round to guess.)

$9 \times 80 = 720$

Write 8 over the tens column.

$$\begin{array}{r} 8 \\ 9\overline{)782} \\ -72\downarrow \\ \hline 62 \end{array}$$

What number times 9 is closest to, but less than or equal to, 62? (Round to guess.)

$9 \times 6 = 54$

$$\begin{array}{r} 8 \\ 9\overline{)782} \\ -72 \\ \hline 62 \\ -54 \\ \hline \text{remainder } 8 \end{array}$$

86 R8
$9\overline{)782}$

1. $5\overline{)86}$

2. $2\overline{)67}$

3. $8\overline{)14}$

4. $7\overline{)79}$

5. $6\overline{)85}$

6. $9\overline{)75}$

7. $3\overline{)467}$

8. $8\overline{)953}$

9. $4\overline{)918}$

Division with Remainders

Solve each problem.

$$
\begin{array}{r}
\mathbf{23}\ \textbf{R5} \\
23\overline{)534} \\
-\,46 \\
\hline
74 \\
-\,69 \\
\hline
5
\end{array}
$$

1. $64\overline{)831}$

2. $44\overline{)641}$

3. $10\overline{)968}$

4. $86\overline{)357}$

5. $42\overline{)118}$

6. $13\overline{)372}$

7. $57\overline{)754}$

8. $61\overline{)789}$

9. $72\overline{)904}$

Division with Remainders

Solve each problem.

121 R12
```
  72)8,724
  - 72
    152
  - 144
     84
   - 72
     12
```

1. 54)2,809

2. 98)9,108

3. 85)3,950

4. 93)7,728

5. 87)6,014

6. 76)6,975

7. 32)2,544

8. 74)4,096

Problem Solving

Solve each problem.

1. Leslie typed 4 articles for her magazine. If each article had 1,432 words, how many words did she type altogether?

2. Carlos proofread 7 stories for his magazine. If each story had 304 paragraphs, how many paragraphs did Carlos proofread altogether?

3. Jamie read 8 magazines for a total of 992 pages. If each magazine had the same number of pages, how many pages are in each magazine?

4. Tyler wrote 5 articles for the newspaper. Each article has the same number of words. If Tyler wrote 2,320 words in all, how many words are in each article?

Prime Factorization

Use a factor tree to find the prime factors.

A **prime number** is a whole number that has only two factors, itself and 1.

Any number that is not a prime number is a **composite number**. **Prime factorization** is finding the prime factors of a number.

To find the prime factors of 24, start with any two factors that equal 24.

The prime factors of 24 are 3, 2, 2, and 2.

$24 = 3 \times 2 \times 2 \times 2$

1. 21

2. 15

3. 55

4. 16

5. 50

6. 18

7. 40

8. 32

9. 24

Equivalent Fractions

Circle the equivalent fractions.

To **rename** a
fraction, multiply
the numerator and
denominator by
the same number.

$\frac{1}{3}$ of the circle
is shaded

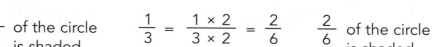

$\frac{1}{3} = \frac{1 \times 2}{3 \times 2} = \frac{2}{6}$

$\frac{2}{6}$ of the circle
is shaded

1. $\frac{7}{10} =$ $\frac{1}{4}$ $\frac{14}{20}$ $\frac{3}{21}$ $\frac{21}{30}$ $\frac{14}{10}$

2. $\frac{3}{8} =$ $\frac{1}{8}$ $\frac{3}{16}$ $\frac{6}{16}$ $\frac{9}{16}$ $\frac{9}{24}$

3. $\frac{1}{2} =$ $\frac{2}{4}$ $\frac{3}{4}$ $\frac{4}{8}$ $\frac{4}{16}$ $\frac{10}{20}$

4. $\frac{2}{3} =$ $\frac{1}{3}$ $\frac{2}{6}$ $\frac{4}{6}$ $\frac{4}{12}$ $\frac{6}{9}$

5. $\frac{2}{5} =$ $\frac{4}{10}$ $\frac{4}{25}$ $\frac{4}{5}$ $\frac{6}{15}$ $\frac{8}{20}$

6. $\frac{1}{8} =$ $\frac{4}{8}$ $\frac{2}{16}$ $\frac{3}{16}$ $\frac{3}{24}$ $\frac{4}{32}$

7. $\frac{1}{4} =$ $\frac{2}{4}$ $\frac{2}{5}$ $\frac{6}{12}$ $\frac{2}{8}$ $\frac{3}{12}$

8. $\frac{1}{6} =$ $\frac{1}{12}$ $\frac{2}{6}$ $\frac{2}{12}$ $\frac{3}{18}$ $\frac{3}{36}$

Renaming Fractions

Complete each equivalent fraction.

$$\frac{4}{5} \longrightarrow \overline{10}$$

To get from 5 to 10, multiply by 2.

$$\frac{4}{5} = \frac{4 \times 2}{5 \times 2} = \frac{8}{10}$$

$$\frac{2}{3} \longrightarrow \overline{12}$$

To get from 3 to 12, multiply by 4.

$$\frac{2}{3} = \frac{2 \times 4}{3 \times 4} = \frac{8}{12}$$

1. $\dfrac{1}{9} = \dfrac{5}{}$ 2. $\dfrac{2}{11} = \dfrac{8}{}$ 3. $\dfrac{}{2} = \dfrac{8}{16}$

4. $\dfrac{1}{4} = \dfrac{}{32}$ 5. $\dfrac{4}{16} = \dfrac{1}{}$ 6. $\dfrac{2}{3} = \dfrac{24}{}$

7. $\dfrac{1}{} = \dfrac{3}{27}$ 8. $\dfrac{5}{} = \dfrac{25}{30}$ 9. $\dfrac{18}{45} = \dfrac{2}{}$

10. $\dfrac{1}{2} = \dfrac{24}{}$ 11. $\dfrac{}{7} = \dfrac{18}{63}$ 12. $\dfrac{6}{} = \dfrac{12}{14}$

Simplifying Fractions

Write each fraction in simplest form.

$$\frac{4}{8} = \frac{4 \div 4}{8 \div 4}$$

$$\frac{4}{8} = \frac{1}{2}$$

A fraction is **simplified** when 1 is the only number that divides into both the numerator and the denominator.

To simplify, you must divide the numerator and denominator by the same number.

1. $\frac{3}{6}$ =

2. $\frac{6}{15}$ =

3. $\frac{8}{24}$ =

4. $\frac{4}{6}$ =

5. $\frac{5}{15}$ =

6. $\frac{6}{10}$ =

7. $\frac{6}{8}$ =

8. $\frac{2}{24}$ =

9. $\frac{8}{12}$ =

10. $\frac{3}{9}$ =

11. $\frac{6}{24}$ =

12. $\frac{10}{12}$ =

Writing Improper Fractions as Mixed Numbers

Write each improper fraction as a simplified mixed number.

$\frac{14}{5}$ is an **improper fraction**. It can be written as $14 \div 5$ or $5)\overline{14}$.	To write an improper fraction as a mixed number, divide the numerator by the denominator. $$\begin{array}{r} 2 \text{ R4} \\ 5\overline{)14} \\ -10 \\ \hline 4 \end{array}$$	$\frac{14}{5} = 2\frac{4}{5}$ The 2 becomes the whole number. The 4 becomes the numerator of the fraction. The denominator is still 5.

1. $\frac{14}{3} =$

2. $\frac{16}{5} =$

3. $\frac{13}{5} =$

4. $\frac{9}{8} =$

5. $\frac{13}{8} =$

6. $\frac{21}{6} =$

7. $\frac{19}{3} =$

8. $\frac{7}{5} =$

9. $\frac{10}{4} =$

10. $\frac{11}{5} =$

11. $\frac{8}{7} =$

12. $\frac{12}{5} =$

13. $\frac{15}{7} =$

14. $\frac{19}{17} =$

15. $\frac{17}{8} =$

Writing Mixed Numbers as Improper Fractions

Write each mixed number as a simplified improper fraction.

$$3\frac{1}{3} = \frac{(3 \times 3) + 1}{3}$$

$$= \frac{9 + 1}{3}$$

$$= \frac{10}{3}$$

To change a mixed number to an improper fraction:
1. Multiply the denominator by the whole number.
2. Add the numerator.
3. Keep the denominator.

1. $4\frac{2}{3} =$

2. $4\frac{3}{4} =$

3. $3\frac{1}{5} =$

4. $3\frac{1}{3} =$

5. $6\frac{1}{3} =$

6. $6\frac{1}{2} =$

7. $1\frac{3}{4} =$

8. $1\frac{5}{8} =$

9. $2\frac{7}{8} =$

10. $3\frac{2}{3} =$

11. $1\frac{1}{2} =$

12. $4\frac{5}{6} =$

13. $5\frac{1}{5} =$

14. $1\frac{7}{16} =$

Least Common Denominators

Find the least common denominator of each pair of fractions.

The **least common denominator (LCD)** for two fractions is the least common multiple of the denominators.

To find the LCD, list the multiples of each denominator. The LCD is the least common multiple.

Find the LCD of $\frac{2}{3}$ and $\frac{3}{4}$.

1. List the multiples of each denominator.
    3 = 3, 6, 9, (12,) 15, 18, 21, 24, . . .
    4 = 4, 8, (12,) 16, 20, 24, . . .

2. The LCD = **12**.

1. $\frac{2}{3}$, $\frac{4}{5}$

2. $\frac{1}{2}$, $\frac{1}{3}$

3. $\frac{2}{5}$, $\frac{1}{2}$

4. $\frac{3}{4}$, $\frac{1}{5}$

5. $\frac{1}{7}$, $\frac{2}{3}$

6. $\frac{6}{11}$, $\frac{1}{3}$

7. $\frac{1}{2}$, $\frac{3}{5}$

8. $\frac{4}{7}$, $\frac{1}{2}$

9. $\frac{2}{3}$, $\frac{5}{8}$

Adding Fractions

Solve each problem. Simplify if possible.

When adding fractions with like denominators:

$$\begin{array}{r} \frac{2}{5} \\ + \ \frac{1}{5} \\ \hline \frac{3}{5} \end{array}$$

1. Add the numerators.
2. Keep the same denominator.
3. Simplify if possible.

1. $$\begin{array}{r} \frac{3}{5} \\ + \ \frac{1}{5} \\ \hline \end{array}$$

2. $$\begin{array}{r} \frac{1}{3} \\ + \ \frac{1}{3} \\ \hline \end{array}$$

3. $$\begin{array}{r} \frac{1}{6} \\ + \ \frac{3}{6} \\ \hline \end{array}$$

4. $$\begin{array}{r} \frac{1}{9} \\ + \ \frac{2}{9} \\ \hline \end{array}$$

5. $$\begin{array}{r} \frac{1}{7} \\ + \ \frac{2}{7} \\ \hline \end{array}$$

6. $$\begin{array}{r} \frac{1}{4} \\ + \ \frac{1}{4} \\ \hline \end{array}$$

7. $$\begin{array}{r} \frac{1}{12} \\ + \ \frac{4}{12} \\ \hline \end{array}$$

8. $$\begin{array}{r} \frac{3}{10} \\ + \ \frac{4}{10} \\ \hline \end{array}$$

9. $$\begin{array}{r} \frac{3}{6} \\ + \ \frac{2}{6} \\ \hline \end{array}$$

10. $$\begin{array}{r} \frac{1}{11} \\ + \ \frac{3}{11} \\ \hline \end{array}$$

11. $$\begin{array}{r} \frac{3}{8} \\ + \ \frac{3}{8} \\ \hline \end{array}$$

12. $$\begin{array}{r} \frac{4}{9} \\ + \ \frac{3}{9} \\ \hline \end{array}$$

Subtracting Fractions

Solve each problem. Simplify if possible.

When subtracting fractions with like denominators:

$$\frac{7}{8}$$
$$-\frac{3}{8}$$
$$\frac{4}{8} = \frac{1}{2}$$

1. Subtract the numerators.
2. Keep the same denominator.
3. Simplify if possible.

1. $\frac{3}{8}$
    $-\frac{1}{8}$

2. $\frac{7}{12}$
    $-\frac{5}{12}$

3. $\frac{5}{6}$
    $-\frac{1}{6}$

4. $\frac{6}{7}$
    $-\frac{3}{7}$

5. $\frac{11}{12}$
    $-\frac{1}{12}$

6. $\frac{9}{10}$
    $-\frac{3}{10}$

7. $\frac{4}{5}$
    $-\frac{2}{5}$

8. $\frac{2}{3}$
    $-\frac{1}{3}$

9. $\frac{3}{4}$
    $-\frac{1}{4}$

Adding Fractions
with Unlike Denominators

Solve each problem. Simplify if possible.

When adding fractions with unlike denominators:

$$\frac{5}{6} \longrightarrow \frac{5 \times 5}{6 \times 5} \longrightarrow \frac{25}{30}$$

$$+\ \frac{2}{5} \longrightarrow \frac{2 \times 6}{5 \times 6} \longrightarrow \frac{12}{30}$$

$$\frac{37}{30}$$

$$= 1\frac{7}{30}$$

1. Find the least common denominator (LCD).
2. Rewrite each fraction using the LCD.
3. Add.
4. Simplify if possible.

1.
$$\frac{3}{8}$$
$$+\ \frac{1}{3}$$

2.
$$\frac{1}{2}$$
$$+\ \frac{1}{3}$$

3.
$$\frac{3}{4}$$
$$+\ \frac{3}{5}$$

4.
$$\frac{1}{3}$$
$$+\ \frac{5}{8}$$

5.
$$\frac{1}{3}$$
$$+\ \frac{3}{4}$$

6.
$$\frac{7}{10}$$
$$+\ \frac{2}{3}$$

Subtracting Fractions with Unlike Denominators

Solve each problem. Simplify if possible.

When subtracting fractions with unlike denominators:

$$\frac{7}{12} \longrightarrow \frac{7}{12}$$

$$-\frac{1}{4} \longrightarrow \frac{1 \times 3}{4 \times 3} \longrightarrow \frac{3}{12}$$

$$\frac{4}{12} = \frac{1}{3}$$

1. Find the least common denominator (LCD).
2. Rewrite each fraction using the LCD.
3. Subtract.
4. Simplify if possible.

1.
$$\frac{3}{4}$$
$$-\frac{7}{10}$$

2.
$$\frac{7}{9}$$
$$-\frac{1}{6}$$

3.
$$\frac{1}{2}$$
$$-\frac{3}{8}$$

4.
$$\frac{2}{3}$$
$$-\frac{2}{9}$$

5.
$$\frac{7}{12}$$
$$-\frac{1}{4}$$

6.
$$\frac{7}{10}$$
$$-\frac{1}{2}$$

Adding Mixed Numbers with Unlike Denominators

Solve each problem. Simplify if possible.

When adding mixed numbers with unlike denominators:

$$2\frac{1}{3} \longrightarrow \frac{1 \times 4}{3 \times 4} \longrightarrow \frac{4}{12}$$

$$3\frac{3}{4} \longrightarrow \frac{3 \times 3}{4 \times 3} \longrightarrow \frac{9}{12}$$

$$+$$

$$5 \qquad\qquad\qquad \frac{13}{12} = 1\frac{1}{12}$$

$$5 + 1\frac{1}{12} = 6\frac{1}{12}$$

1. Add the whole numbers.
2. Find the least common denominator (LCD).
3. Rewrite each fraction using the LCD.
4. Add.
5. Simplify if possible.

1. $5\frac{1}{3}$
   $+\ 1\frac{5}{6}$

2. $3\frac{2}{3}$
   $+\ 2\frac{1}{4}$

3. $6\frac{1}{2}$
   $+\ 1\frac{3}{4}$

4. $5\frac{2}{5}$
   $+\ 2\frac{1}{3}$

5. $4\frac{1}{6}$
   $+\ 2\frac{3}{4}$

6. $1\frac{7}{8}$
   $+\ 2\frac{1}{6}$

Subtracting Mixed Numbers

Solve each problem. Simplify if possible.

Rewrite $3\dfrac{1}{4}$ so that you can subtract.

$$3\dfrac{1}{4} = 2 + 1\dfrac{1}{4} = 2\dfrac{5}{4}$$

$$-\ 1\dfrac{3}{4} \longrightarrow -\ 1\dfrac{3}{4}$$

$$1\dfrac{2}{4} = 1\dfrac{1}{2}$$

1. $3\dfrac{3}{7}$

    $-\ 1\dfrac{5}{7}$

2. $5\dfrac{1}{3}$

    $-\ 2\dfrac{2}{3}$

3. $4\dfrac{1}{6}$

    $-\ 3\dfrac{5}{6}$

4. $8\dfrac{3}{8}$

    $-\ 2\dfrac{5}{8}$

5. $6\dfrac{1}{5}$

    $-\ 3\dfrac{3}{5}$

6. $4\dfrac{3}{10}$

    $-\ 3\dfrac{7}{10}$

Problem Solving

Solve each problem. Simplify if possible. Write improper fractions as mixed numbers.

1. Jason used $\frac{2}{3}$ yard of string for his kite. Then, he used another $\frac{5}{8}$ yard. How many yards of string did Jason use altogether?

2. Katie bought $2\frac{1}{4}$ yards of fabric for her project. She used $\frac{1}{3}$ yard of fabric. How many yards of fabric does she have left?

3. Deanna measured $\frac{3}{4}$ yard of ribbon. Then, she measured $\frac{5}{6}$ yard more. How many yards of ribbon did she measure altogether?

4. Connor bought a piece of wood that measured $7\frac{1}{3}$ feet. He cut off a piece that measured $1\frac{5}{7}$ feet. How long is the piece that he has left?

Multiplying Fractions

Solve each problem. Simplify if possible.

When multiplying fractions:
1. Multiply the numerators.
2. Multiply the denominators.
3. Simplify if possible.

$$\frac{3}{4} \times \frac{4}{5} = \frac{3 \times 4}{4 \times 5}$$
$$= \frac{12}{20}$$
$$= \frac{3}{5}$$

1. $\dfrac{3}{8} \times \dfrac{2}{3} =$

2. $\dfrac{4}{5} \times \dfrac{1}{2} =$

3. $\dfrac{1}{3} \times \dfrac{6}{7} =$

4. $\dfrac{2}{3} \times \dfrac{5}{6} =$

5. $\dfrac{1}{3} \times \dfrac{3}{10} =$

6. $\dfrac{4}{9} \times \dfrac{3}{4} =$

7. $\dfrac{3}{8} \times \dfrac{1}{6} =$

8. $\dfrac{2}{3} \times \dfrac{6}{7} =$

9. $\dfrac{5}{6} \times \dfrac{1}{10} =$

Multiplying Fractions

Solve each problem. Simplify if possible.

When multiplying a whole number and a fraction:

1. Rewrite the whole number as a fraction with a denominator of 1.

2. Multiply the numerators.

3. Multiply the denominators.

4. Simplify if possible.

$$\frac{3}{4} \times 6 = \frac{3}{4} \times \frac{6}{1}$$

$$= \frac{3 \times 6}{4 \times 1}$$

$$= \frac{18}{4}$$

$$= 4\frac{2}{4} = \mathbf{4\frac{1}{2}}$$

1. $3 \times \dfrac{2}{3} =$

2. $\dfrac{4}{5} \times 2 =$

3. $1 \times \dfrac{6}{7} =$

4. $2 \times \dfrac{4}{7} =$

5. $\dfrac{2}{5} \times 6 =$

6. $3 \times \dfrac{3}{10} =$

7. $9 \times \dfrac{3}{4} =$

8. $6 \times \dfrac{3}{10} =$

9. $8 \times \dfrac{1}{6} =$

Multiplying Mixed Numbers

Solve each problem. Simplify if possible.

When multiplying a mixed number and a fraction:

1. Rewrite the mixed number as an improper fraction.
2. Multiply the numerators.
3. Multiply the denominators.
4. Simplify if possible.

$$\frac{1}{3} \times 2\frac{2}{3} = \frac{1}{3} \times \frac{8}{3}$$

$$= \frac{1 \times 8}{3 \times 3}$$

$$= \frac{8}{9}$$

1. $\frac{1}{2} \times 1\frac{1}{8} =$

2. $2\frac{1}{3} \times \frac{1}{3} =$

3. $4\frac{1}{2} \times \frac{1}{3} =$

4. $2\frac{2}{3} \times \frac{3}{7} =$

5. $3\frac{1}{2} \times \frac{1}{4} =$

6. $\frac{3}{5} \times 3\frac{1}{2} =$

7. $\frac{2}{5} \times 3\frac{1}{3} =$

8. $\frac{2}{3} \times 5\frac{1}{4} =$

9. $4\frac{3}{4} \times \frac{1}{3} =$

Decimal Place Value

Write the missing numbers for the decimal values in the chart below.

	Ones		Tenths	Hundredths	Thousandths
four hundredths	0	.	0	4	0
six thousandths		.			
thirty-six thousandths		.			
ten hundredths		.			
twenty-seven thousandths		.			
ninety-two hundredths		.			
forty-seven thousandths		.			
eighty-nine hundredths		.			
two tenths		.			
eight hundredths		.			

Decimal Place Value

Write each decimal.

Just like there are place value names for numbers larger than 0, there are also names for place values after the decimal point.

Decimal	Read As	Equivalent Fraction
0.7	seven tenths	$\frac{7}{10}$
0.23	twenty-three hundredths	$\frac{23}{100}$
0.045	forty-five thousandths	$\frac{45}{1000}$
15.01	fifteen and one hundredth	$15\frac{1}{100}$

1. 3 and 6 tenths

   _____

2. 6 and 1 hundredth

   _____

3. 1 and 8 hundredths

   _____

4. 7 and 2 tenths

   _____

5. 3 and 32 thousandths

   _____

6. 4 and 2 thousandths

   _____

7. $108\frac{7}{10}$ = _____

8. $64\frac{2}{100}$ = _____

9. $82\frac{5}{100}$ = _____

10. $81\frac{5}{10}$ = _____

11. $42\frac{93}{1000}$ = _____

12. $11\frac{27}{100}$ = _____

Rounding Decimals

Round each number to the nearest tenth.

2.07 ___**2.1**___   1. 5.67 _____   2. 7.38 _____

3. 5.42 _____   4. 8.61 _____   5. 33.01 _____

6. 7.39 _____   7. 68.96 _____   8. 4.97 _____

9. 26.55 _____   10. 122.18 _____   11. 80.83 _____

Round each number to the nearest hundredth.

12. 3.047 _____   13. 9.921 _____   14. 8.043 _____

15. 62.686 _____   16. 4.769 _____   17. 27.977 _____

18. 1.588 _____   19. 5.815 _____   20. 3.251 _____

21. 51.971 _____   22. 81.745 _____   23. 6.378 _____

Comparing Decimals

Compare each pair of numbers. Use >, <, or =.

When comparing decimals, line up the numbers by place value. Then, compare the digits left to right.

0.07 ◯ 0.7

1. Line up: 0.07
            0.7

2. Compare. After the decimal points, you have 0 and 7. 7 is greater than 0, so 0.7 is greater.

0.07 ⊘< 0.7

1. 0.007 ◯ 0.07

2. 0.08 ◯ 0.8

3. 101.05 ◯ 101.005

4. 10.05 ◯ 10.005

5. 0.99 ◯ 0.009

6. 214.01 ◯ 214.001

7. 30.249 ◯ 30.429

8. 9.008 ◯ 9.08

9. 614.05 ◯ 614.05

10. 6.041 ◯ 6.401

11. 8.26 ◯ 8.026

12. 92.001 ◯ 92.001

13. 43.014 ◯ 43.104

14. 263.08 ◯ 263.81

Comparing and Ordering Decimals

Write the prices on the menu in order from least to greatest.

$1.25 $2.03 $1.07 $2.51 $1.10 $2.15 $2.21 $1.05

Item:	Price:
Soda	
Milk	
Fries	
Salad	
Cheese Sandwich	
Tuna Sandwich	
Hamburger	
Cheeseburger	

Circle the largest number in each row.

1.   4.05   4.50   4.005   4.15

2.   10.57   10.49   10.005   10.057

3.   2.5   2.15   2.52   2.005

4.   1.8   1.84   1.48   1.847

5.   89.90   88.19   8.90   89.09

Adding and Subtracting Decimals

Solve each problem. Write the letter from the box on the line below that matches the answer.

$$\begin{array}{r} \overset{1\ 1\ 1}{26.53} \\ +\ 17.49 \\ \hline \mathbf{44.02} \end{array}$$

1.
$$\begin{array}{r} 64.42 \\ +\ 6.70 \\ \hline \end{array}$$

A

2.
$$\begin{array}{r} 57.10 \\ +\ 43.99 \\ \hline \end{array}$$

C

3.
$$\begin{array}{r} 248.80 \\ -\ 57.98 \\ \hline \end{array}$$

T

4.
$$\begin{array}{r} 100.3 \\ -\ 78.87 \\ \hline \end{array}$$

H

5.
$$\begin{array}{r} 123.50 \\ +\ 64.75 \\ \hline \end{array}$$

E

6.
$$\begin{array}{r} 454.6 \\ -\ 56.8 \\ \hline \end{array}$$

E

7.
$$\begin{array}{r} 84.96 \\ +\ 86.75 \\ \hline \end{array}$$

H

This is the fastest land animal, with a speed of more than 60 miles (97 km) per hour.

$\overline{\text{101.09}}$ $\overline{\text{21.43}}$ $\overline{\text{188.25}}$ $\overline{\text{397.8}}$ $\overline{\text{190.82}}$ $\overline{\text{71.12}}$ $\overline{\text{171.71}}$

Adding and Subtracting Decimals

Solve each problem. Write the letter from the box on the line below that matches the answer.

1.   917.42
     + 32.70
	2. 52.10
	     − 33.76
		3. 566.50
		     + 512.65

R	**G**	**A**

4.   207.4
     − 67.57
	5. 75.100
	     + 75.867
		6. 257.30
		     + 65.82

O	**D**	**N**

7.   267.50
     − 176.88
	8. 798.52
	     + 357.90
		9. 9.008
		     − 8.789

F	**Y**	**L**

This is the fastest flying insect, with a speed of approximately 35 miles (56 km) per hour.

————— ————— ————— ————— ————— ————— ————— ————— —————
150.967 950.12 1,079.15 18.34 139.83 323.12 90.62 0.219 1,156.42

Multiplying Decimals

Solve each problem.

To multiply decimals, multiply as you would with whole numbers. Then, count the total number of decimal places to the right of the decimal point in both factors. That is the number of decimal places in the product.

$$
\begin{array}{r}
2.53 \leftarrow \text{2 decimal places} \\
\times\ 3.1 \leftarrow + \text{1 decimal place} \\
\hline
253 \\
+\ 7590 \\
\hline
7.843 \leftarrow \text{3 decimal places}
\end{array}
$$

1.
$$
\begin{array}{r}
2.64 \\
\times\quad 9 \\
\hline
\end{array}
$$

2.
$$
\begin{array}{r}
6.48 \\
\times\quad 7 \\
\hline
\end{array}
$$

3.
$$
\begin{array}{r}
12.9 \\
\times\quad 17 \\
\hline
\end{array}
$$

4.
$$
\begin{array}{r}
54.87 \\
\times\quad 24 \\
\hline
\end{array}
$$

5.
$$
\begin{array}{r}
3.348 \\
\times\quad 63 \\
\hline
\end{array}
$$

6.
$$
\begin{array}{r}
4.05 \\
\times\quad 69 \\
\hline
\end{array}
$$

7.
$$
\begin{array}{r}
2.469 \\
\times\quad 236 \\
\hline
\end{array}
$$

8.
$$
\begin{array}{r}
9.12 \\
\times\quad 4.3 \\
\hline
\end{array}
$$

9.
$$
\begin{array}{r}
10.16 \\
\times\quad 2.21 \\
\hline
\end{array}
$$

Multiplying Decimals

Solve each problem.

1.
$$
\begin{array}{r}
0.7 \\
\times\ 0.4 \\
\hline
\end{array}
$$

2.
$$
\begin{array}{r}
0.54 \\
\times\ 0.6 \\
\hline
\end{array}
$$

3.
$$
\begin{array}{r}
2.9 \\
\times\ 5.4 \\
\hline
\end{array}
$$

4.
$$
\begin{array}{r}
8.4 \\
\times\ 6 \\
\hline
\end{array}
$$

5.
$$
\begin{array}{r}
0.12 \\
\times\ 0.07 \\
\hline
\end{array}
$$

6.
$$
\begin{array}{r}
0.724 \\
\times\ 0.6 \\
\hline
\end{array}
$$

7.
$$
\begin{array}{r}
0.46 \\
\times\ 0.87 \\
\hline
\end{array}
$$

8.
$$
\begin{array}{r}
71.865 \\
\times\ 45 \\
\hline
\end{array}
$$

9.
$$
\begin{array}{r}
98.077 \\
\times\ 45 \\
\hline
\end{array}
$$

Dividing Decimals

Solve each problem.

Perform division as if there is no decimal point in the dividend.

```
    1 73
5) 8.65
  - 5
    36
   - 35
     15
    - 15
      0
```

Then, write a decimal point in the quotient directly above the decimal point in the dividend.

```
    1.73
5) 8.65
```

$8.65 \div 5 = 1.73$

1. $6\overline{)25.50}$

2. $7\overline{)3.99}$

3. $3\overline{)83.7}$

4. $4\overline{)49.12}$

5. $8\overline{)1.96}$

6. $7\overline{)55.86}$

7. $4\overline{)3.04}$

8. $2\overline{)1.826}$

9. $9\overline{)5.526}$

Dividing Decimals by Decimals

Solve each problem.

$$1.32\overline{)35.772}$$

Multiply both the divisor and the dividend by a multiple of 10 to make the divisor a whole number. $1.32 \times 100 = 132$ $3577.2 \times 100 = 3577.2$	Move the decimal point in the dividend the same number of places. $1.32\overline{)35.772}$ Place the decimal point in the quotient. $132\overline{)3577.2}$	Divide. $\begin{array}{r} 27.1 \\ 132\overline{)3577.2} \\ -\,246 \\ \hline 937 \\ -\,924 \\ \hline 132 \\ -\,132 \\ \hline 0 \end{array}$

1. $0.2\overline{)17.8}$

2. $3.4\overline{)80.24}$

3. $2.5\overline{)114.75}$

4. $1.9\overline{)149.72}$

5. $3.8\overline{)262.58}$

6. $5.1\overline{)196.86}$

Fractions and Percents

The number 100 is used in ratios called **percents**. *Percent* means "per 100."

To change a fraction to a percent, convert a fraction in simplest form to a fraction with a denominator of 100. Once you have solved for the numerator, add a percent sign (%) after it. Delete the denominator.

$$\frac{3}{4} = \frac{n}{100} \qquad \frac{3 \times 25}{4 \times 25} = \frac{\textbf{75}}{\textbf{100}} = 75\%$$

To change a percent to a fraction, write the percent over 100. Delete the percent sign. Then, simplify the fraction if possible.

$$75\% = \frac{75}{100} = \frac{\textbf{3}}{\textbf{4}}$$

Write each fraction as a percent.

1. $\frac{9}{100} =$

2. $\frac{1}{25} =$

3. $\frac{3}{10} =$

4. $\frac{1}{2} =$

5. $\frac{4}{5} =$

6. $\frac{1}{10} =$

Write each percent as a fraction with 100 as the denominator and as a simplified fraction.

	Percent	25%	3%	50%	33%	65%	56%	30%	5%
7.	Equivalent Fraction	$\frac{25}{100}$	$\frac{3}{100}$						
8.	Fraction in Simplest Form	$\frac{1}{4}$	$\frac{3}{100}$						

Fractions, Decimals, and Percents

Write the missing fraction, decimal, or percent.

To write a fraction as a decimal, divide the numerator by the denominator.

$\dfrac{5}{8} = 5 \div 8 = \mathbf{0.625}$

To change a decimal to a percent, multiply by 100. Then, write a percent sign.

$0.36 \times 100 = \mathbf{36\%}$ $0.04 \times 100 = \mathbf{4\%}$ $0.152 \times 100 = \mathbf{15.2\%}$

To change a percent to a decimal, divide by 100 and delete the percent sign.

$42\% \div 100 = \mathbf{0.42}$ $9\% \div 100 = \mathbf{0.09}$ $2.35\% \div 100 = \mathbf{0.235}$

To write a decimal as a fraction, make the digits to the right of the decimal point the numerator. The place value of the numbers to the right of the decimal point determine the denominator.

$0.15 = \dfrac{15}{100}$

Fraction	Decimal	Percent
$\dfrac{5}{100}$	**0.05**	**5%**
1.		14%
2. $\dfrac{27}{100}$		
3.		32%
4.	0.89	
5.		57%

Fraction	Decimal	Percent
6.	0.17	
7. $\dfrac{71}{100}$		
8.		43%
9.	0.34	
10. $\dfrac{64}{100}$		
11.	0.75	

Comparing Integers

Compare each pair of integers. Write >, <, or =.

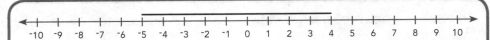

4 > -5 A positive number is always greater than a negative number. The integer with the greatest value is the number farthest to the right on a number line.

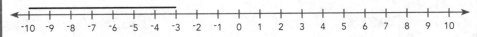

-3 > -10 With two negative numbers, the greater number is the integer closer to 0.

1. -5 ◯ -2

2. 10 ◯ -2

3. -4 ◯ 3

4. 8 ◯ 2

5. 9 ◯ 3

6. 7 ◯ -12

7. 10 ◯ 10

8. 2 ◯ -12

9. 3 ◯ -3

10. -5 ◯ 1

11. -6 ◯ 2

12. -8 ◯ 10

Adding Integers

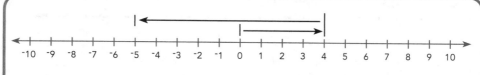

$$4 + (-9) = -5$$

Begin at zero. 4 is a positive integer, so move to the right 4 steps. Then, move to the left 9 steps. The sum is -5.

Positive integers move to the right.

Negative integers move to the left.

Use the number line to find each sum.

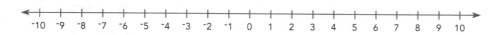

1. 8 + (-7) = ___

2. -3 + 4 = _____

3. -9 + (-2) = ___

4. 7 + 2 = _____

5. -11 + 2 = ____

6. 9 + (-10) = ___

7. -4 + 7 = _____

8. -6 + 4 = _____

9. 8 + 6 = _____

10. -4 + 9 = _____

11. 3 + (-2) = ___

12. -9 + 2 = _____

Circle the equation shown on the number line. Solve.

13.

A. 2 + (-5) = _____

B. -5 + 7 = _____

C. -5 + 2 = _____

D. 7 + 2 = _____

Solving Equations with Variables

Find the value of each variable.

To solve for the variable, always use the inverse operation on both sides of the equation.	$m - 6 = 10$ $6 + m - 6 = 10 + 6$ Add 6 to both sides.	Add. $m = \mathbf{10 + 6}$ $m = \mathbf{16}$

1. $a + 5 = 15$

2. $c + 14 = 20$

3. $e + 6 = 26$

4. $g + 3.2 = 6.8$

5. $i - 1.3 = 10.5$

6. $k - 3.9 = 11.1$

7. $m - 22 = 46$

8. $b - 4 = 9$

9. $d + 3 = 7$

10. $f - 1.4 = 9.6$

11. $h + 3.6 = 8.6$

12. $j + 6.6 = 9.5$

Coordinate Graphing

Plot and label the points on the coordinate plane. The first number is how far left or right. The second number is how far up or down.

A. (5,3)

B. (-4,-2)

C. (3,2)

D. (0,-4)

E. (-4,1)

F. (2,-3)

G. (2,-1)

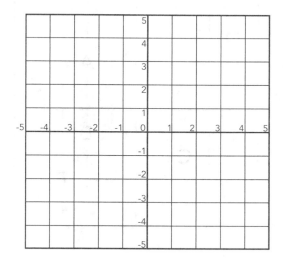

Use the coordinate plane to fill in the missing coordinates.

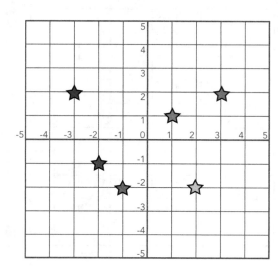

1. ⭐ (___, ___)

2. ☆ (___, ___)

3. ⭐ (___, ___)

4. ⭐ (___, ___)

5. ⭐ (___, ___)

6. ⭐ (___, ___)

Coordinate Graphing

Use the coordinate plane to fill in the missing coordinates.

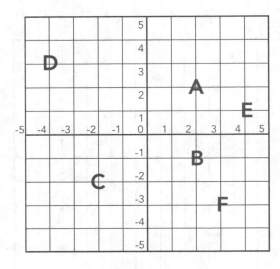

1. A (_____, _____)

2. B (_____, _____)

3. C (_____, _____)

4. D (_____, _____)

5. E (_____, _____)

6. F (_____, _____)

Plot and label the points on the coordinate plane.

G. (-1,4)

H. (5,4)

I. (0,-2)

J. (-3,1)

K. (3,3)

L. (-4,-3)

M. (2,-3)

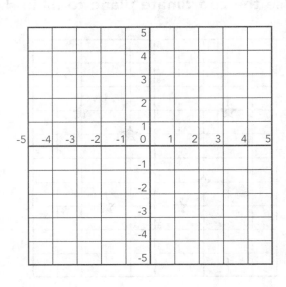

Customary Length

1 ft. = 12 in.

1 yd. = 3 ft.

1 mi. = 5,280 ft.

To convert a smaller unit to a larger unit, divide.	To convert a larger unit to a smaller unit, multiply.
48 in. = _____ ft.	3 ft. = _____ in.
48 in. = (48 ÷ 12) ft. = **4 ft.**	3 ft. = (3 × 12) in. = **36 in.**

Circle the best answer.

1. the length of a desk   3 in.   3 ft.   3 yd.   3 mi.

2. the length of a pencil   8 in.   8 ft.   8 yd.   8 mi.

3. the height of a school   7 in.   7 ft.   7 yd.   7 mi.

Convert each measurement.

4. 60 in. = _____ ft.

5. 5 ft. = _____ in.

6. 4 yd. 2 ft. = _____ ft.

7. 2 mi. = _____ ft.

8. 7 ft. 3 in. = _____ in.

9. 3 mi. 310 ft. = _____ ft.

10. 13 ft. 2 in. = _____ in.

11. 21 yd. 6 ft. = _____ ft.

Metric Length

1 km = 1,000 m

1 m = 100 cm

1 cm = 10 mm

---

1 **millimeter** (mm) is about the width of the head of a pin.

1 **centimeter** (cm) is about the width of your index finger.

1 **meter** (m) is about the length of a baseball bat.

1 **kilometer** (km) is just over a $\frac{1}{2}$ mile.

Circle the best answer.

1. What would you measure the height of a house in?

   mm   cm   m   km

2. What would you measure the height of a tree in?

   mm   cm   m   km

3. What would you measure the length of a spoon in?

   mm   cm   m   km

Convert each measurement.

4. 42 m = _____ cm   5. 4 km = _____ m   6. 85 cm = _____ mm

7. 300 cm = _____ m   8. 800 mm = ___ cm   9. 2,000 m = ___ km

Perimeter

Write the perimeter of each shape.

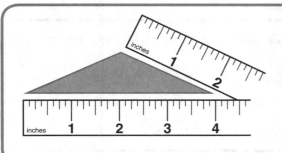

The **perimeter** is the distance around a figure.

Perimeter = 2 + 2 + 4

Perimeter = **8 inches**

1.
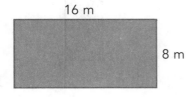
16 m
8 m

_____

2.
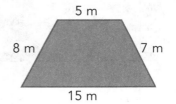
5 m
8 m   7 m
15 m

_____

3.
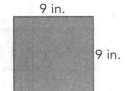
9 in.
9 in.

_____

4.
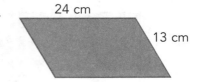
24 cm
13 cm

_____

5.
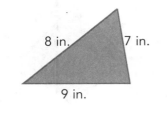
8 in.   7 in.
9 in.

_____

6.
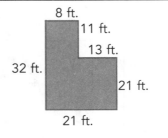
8 ft.
11 ft.
13 ft.
32 ft.
21 ft.
21 ft.

_____

Area

Write the area of each shape.

The **area** of a rectangle is equal to the length times the width.

4 cm

2 cm

$A = l \times w$

$A = 4 \times 2$

$A = \textbf{8 cm}^2$

1.
9 in.

7 in.

_____

2.
5 ft.

11 ft.

_____

3.
12 m

4 m

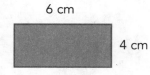

_____

4.
6 cm

4 cm

_____

5.
7 m

11 m

_____

6.
5 in.

5 in.

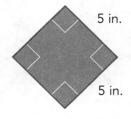

_____

Problem Solving

Solve each problem.

1. Mario measures the bedroom for new carpet. The room measures 14 feet by 27 feet. How much carpet will he need?

2. Nora wants to put new glass in her window. If her window measures 34 inches by 48 inches, what is the area of the glass that she will need?

3. Kendra is building a backyard fence. Two of the sides are 43 feet, and the other two sides are 57 feet. How much fencing does Kendra need?

4. Eric is making a square flower bed in his yard. What is the perimeter of his flower bed if each edge measures 259 inches?

Volume of Rectangular Prisms

Find the volume of each figure.

Volume is the number of cubic units of space inside a figure.

To find the volume, multiply the length times the width times the height.

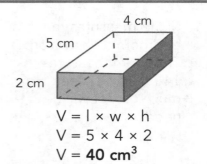

$$V = l \times w \times h$$
$$V = 5 \times 4 \times 2$$
$$V = \mathbf{40 \ cm^3}$$

1.

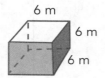

6 m, 6 m, 6 m

V = _____

2.

4 in.
8 in.
5 in.

V = _____

3.

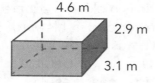

4.6 m, 2.9 m, 3.1 m

V = _____

4.

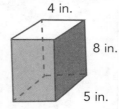

6 mm, 10 mm, 4 mm

V = _____

5. Is 350 cubic feet of air enough to fill this model of a building? Calculate the total volume to find out.

_____

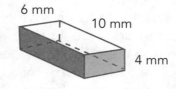
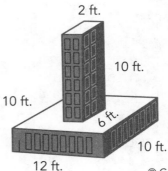

2 ft.
10 ft.
10 ft.
6 ft.
2 ft.
12 ft.
10 ft.

Types of Lines

Circle the term that identifies each figure.

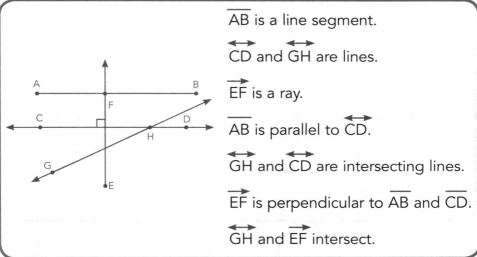

$\overline{AB}$ is a line segment.

$\overleftrightarrow{CD}$ and $\overleftrightarrow{GH}$ are lines.

$\overrightarrow{EF}$ is a ray.

$\overline{AB}$ is parallel to $\overleftrightarrow{CD}$.

$\overleftrightarrow{GH}$ and $\overleftrightarrow{CD}$ are intersecting lines.

$\overrightarrow{EF}$ is perpendicular to $\overline{AB}$ and $\overline{CD}$.

$\overleftrightarrow{GH}$ and $\overrightarrow{EF}$ intersect.

1.   line   line segment   ray

2.   line   line segment   ray

3.   line   line segment   ray

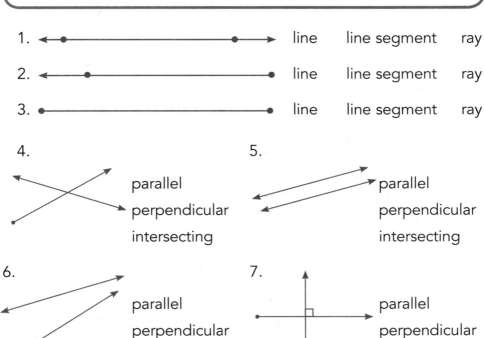

4.

parallel

perpendicular

intersecting

5.

parallel

perpendicular

intersecting

6.

parallel

perpendicular

intersecting

7.

parallel

perpendicular

intersecting

Types of Angles

Write the type of angle shown.

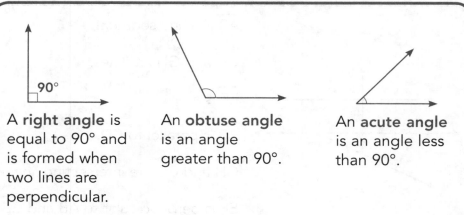

A **right angle** is equal to 90° and is formed when two lines are perpendicular.

An **obtuse angle** is an angle greater than 90°.

An **acute angle** is an angle less than 90°.

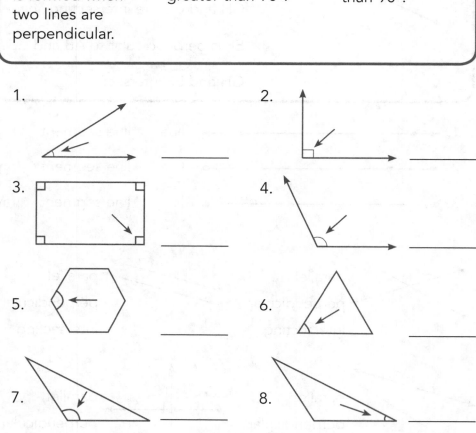

1. _____

2. _____

3. _____

4. _____

5. _____

6. _____

7. _____

8. _____

Congruent and Similar

Classify each pair as similar or congruent.

Congruent polygons have equal side lengths and angles.
Similar polygons have equal angles.

A 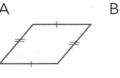 B C D

Parallelograms A and B
are congruent.

Triangles C and D
are similar.

1. 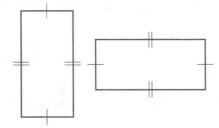   2.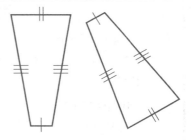

_____   _____

3. 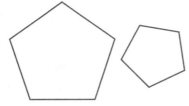   4.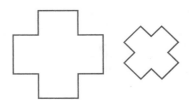

_____   _____

Mean, Median, Mode, and Range

Write the mean, median, mode, and range of each set.

The **mean** is the sum of the items divided by the number of items.

$$\frac{5 + 8 + 3 + 1 + 3}{5} = \frac{20}{5} = 4 \leftarrow \text{mean}$$

The **median** is the middle number when the data are arranged from least to greatest.

1 3 3 5 8   median

The **mode** is the number that occurs most frequently.

1 3 3 5 8   mode

A data set can have more than one mode. However, if no number occurs more frequently than the others, the data set has no mode.

The **range** is the difference between the greatest value and the least value in the data.

$$8 - 1 = 7$$

1.   18, 10, 10, 8, 35, 10, 21

mean: _____   median: _____

mode: _____   range: _____

2.   7, 14, 10, 14, 29, 16, 15

mean: _____   median: _____

mode: _____   range: _____

Reading a Bar Graph

The fifth-grade class at Roosevelt Elementary School recorded the amount of rainfall at the school for four months. Use the bar graph to answer each question.

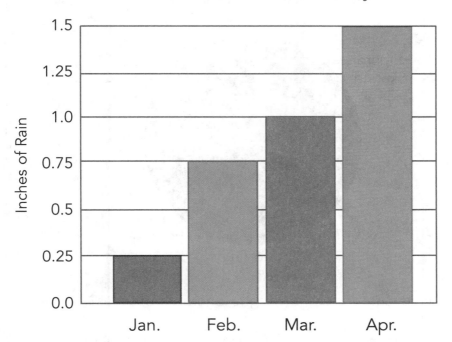

Rainfall at Roosevelt Elementary

1. Which month had the most rain?

2. Which month had the least rain?

3. How many more inches did it rain in April than in March?

4. What was the average amount of rain for January through April?

Reading a Pie Graph

The students at Grant Elementary School voted on their favorite Winter Olympic events. Use the circle graph to answer each question.

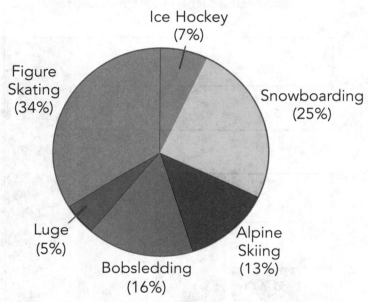

Favorite Winter Olympic Events

Ice Hockey (7%)

Figure Skating (34%)

Snowboarding (25%)

Luge (5%)

Alpine Skiing (13%)

Bobsledding (16%)

1. Which event received the highest number of votes?

2. What percentage of students voted for bobsledding?

3. Which event did 25% of the students vote for as their favorite?

4. What was the total percentage of students that liked the luge or bobsledding?

5. What percentage of students voted for either luge, bobsledding, or alpine skiing as their favorite?

Reading a Line Graph

Best Bargain electronics store tracked its TV sales for seven months. Use the line graph to answer each question.

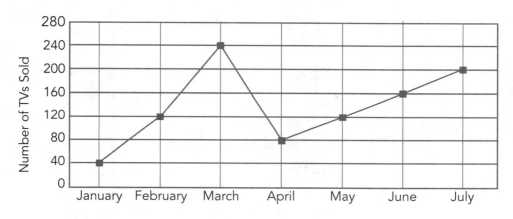

Best Bargain TV Sales

1. In what month were the most TVs sold?

2. In which 2 months were the same number of TVs sold?

3. How many TVs were sold in May?

4. What happened to the number of sales during the months of April through May?

5. How many more TVs were sold in March than in April?

6. What was the average number of TVs sold during January through April? Round your answer to the nearest whole number.

Place Value

Read the clue to write the four-digit number. Change one digit each time to make the next statement true.

1. ___ ___ ___ ___ Write a four-digit number with all even digits that get smaller from left to right. The sum of the digits is 20.

2. ___ ___ ___ ___ This four-digit odd number has a hundreds digit that is one less than the ones digit.

3. ___ ___ ___ ___ This four-digit even number has ones and tens digits that are the same.

4. ___ ___ ___ ___ This four-digit odd number's digits have a sum of 21.

5. ___ ___ ___ ___ This four-digit odd number's thousands digit is twice that of the ones digit.

6. ___ ___ ___ ___ Each digit is one less than the digit to its left in this four-digit number.

7. ___ ___ ___ ___ Sixteen is the sum of the four digits in this odd number. The thousands and tens digits are the same. The difference between the number in the hundreds place and the number in the ones place is 2.

Algebraic Expressions

Write each expression to fill in the missing parts of the table.

Algebraic Expression	Expression in Words
$g - 9$	nine less than g
1.	k divided by five
2.	v and five
3.	y decreased by seven
4.	six times s
5.	twelve divided by j
6.	t less than fifteen
7.	twenty more than c
8. $12e$	
9. $w + 34$	
10. $36 \div m$	
11. $q - 6$	
12. $n - 3$	
13. $7z$	

Three-Dimensional Objects

Match each object with its correct top and side views.

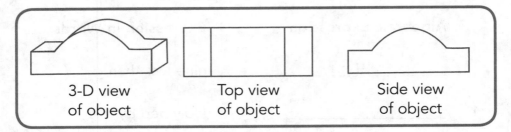

3-D view
of object

Top view
of object

Side view
of object

Top View   Side View

A. 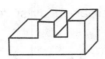 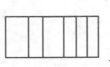 ___  ___

B. 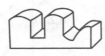 ___ 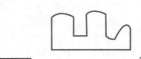 ___

C. 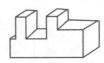 ___ 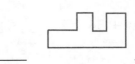 ___

D. 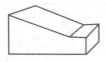 ___ ___

Paths

Solve each problem.

To determine a path's distance, count the blocks traveled to reach the location. The path using the fewest blocks is the path with the shortest distance. The shortest distance from David's house to school is 5 miles. Often, there are several paths of equal distance.

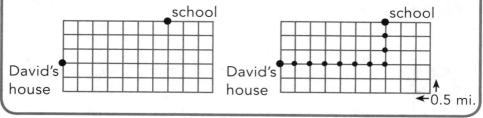

1. Draw three paths from Skate Park to Evan's house to Mark's tree fort. How far is the shortest route?

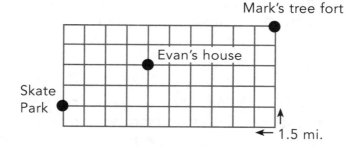

2. Draw a route from the movie theater to Kite Park by way of Martha and Andre's houses. What is the distance?

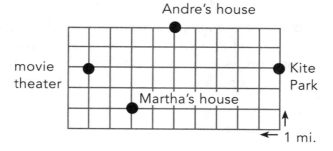

Tabletop Math

Mr. and Mrs. Wood own a furniture store. They have tables of different shapes, but every table has a perimeter of 36 feet. Use the clues to find the lengths of the sides of each table.

1. All of the sides are the same length. Each side is _____ feet long.

2. All of the sides are the same length. Each side is _____ feet long.

3. The length is twice the width. The length is _____ feet and the width is _____ feet.

4. The longest side is 3 feet longer than the second longest side. The second longest side is 3 feet longer than the shortest side. The sides are _____ feet, _____ feet, and _____ feet.

5. Mr. Wood placed rectangular tables that were 8 feet by 10 feet side by side to make one large table. Mrs. Wood did the same. The perimeter of Mr. Wood's large table, though, was less than the perimeter of Mrs. Wood's. How could this be?

74

Creating Graphs

Look at each set of data. Then, choose the best graph type to organize that data set. Enter the data and complete the graph. Label each graph with the appropriate title.

Bar Graph _____

| | | |

Circle Graph _____

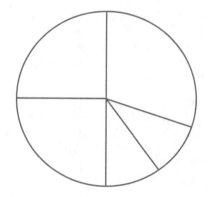

Favorite Subject by Grade Level

Fourth Grade
Science: 50 votes
Math: 70 votes

Fifth Grade
Science: 30 votes
Math: 65 votes

Sixth Grade
Science: 50 votes
Math: 60 votes

Favorite Music

Country	30%
Hip-hop	10%
Classical	10%
Gospel	25%
Rock 'n' roll	25%

Answer Key

Page 3
1. 663,000; 663,300; 2. 164,000; 163,700; 3. 2,000; 2,500; 4. 59,000; 59,400; 5. 82,000; 82,300;
6. 12,000; 12,400; 7. 48,000; 48,400; 8. 111,000; 110,600; 9. 55,000; 54,600; 10. 98,000; 98,400;
11. 2,000; 1,500; 12. 269,000; 268,600; 13. 98,000; 97,800; 14. 104,000; 104,100; 15. 82,000; 82,300; 16. 35,000; 35,400;
17. 122,000; 121,600; 18. 54,000; 53,800; 19. 10,000; 9,600; 20. 84,000; 83,600

Page 4
1. 52,576; 2. 26,915; 3. 434,629; 4. 968,331; 5. 660,182; 6. 933,507; 7. 457,229; 8. 203,874; 9. 40,000 + 6,000 + 200 + 70 + 9; 10. 60,000 + 500 + 40 + 2; 11. 300,000 + 70,000 + 8,000 + 700 + 20; 12. 100,000 + 10,000 + 2,000 + 300 + 5

Page 5
1. 20,731; 2. 34,730; 3. 60,273; 4. 27,694; 5. 16,792; 6. 89,463; 7. 36,835; 8. 230,589; 9. 2,670,409

Page 6
1. >; 2. >; 3. >; 4. >; 5. =; 6. <; 7. >; 8. <; 9. <; 10. <; 11. =; 12. >; 13. >; 14. >; 15. <; 16. =; 17. >

Page 7
1. $10.00; 2. $12.00; 3. $13.00; 4. $11.00; 5. $16.00

Page 8
1. 1,699; 2. 11,661; 3. 13,173; 4. 111,246; 5. 130,430; 6. 110,920; 7. 98,510; 8. 1,561; 9. 710; 10. 1,871; 11. 1,815; 12. 19,454; 13. 15,701; 14. 22,113; 15. 18,740

Page 9
1. 10,918; 2. 105,124; 3. 56,237; 4. 980,774; 5. 170,781; 6. 577,687; 7. 715,363; 8. 1,110,044; 9. 1,061,592; 10. 1,847,386; 11. 1,310,895; 12. 19,553; 13. 28,325; 14. 14,853; 15. 22,444

Page 10
1. 151; 2. 69; 3. 516; 4. 685; 5. 286; 6. 169; 7. 155; 8. 1,594; 9. 4,168; 10. 163; 11. 4,175; 12. 2,582; 13. 1,304; 14. 4,608; 15. 6,885

Page 11
1. 3,856; 2. 5,402; 3. 3,907; 4. 4,487; 5. 6,188; 6. 479; 7. 979; 8. 18,494; 9. 35,356; 10. 34,646; 11. 14,688; 12. 56,197; 13. 84,096; 14. 13,096; 15. 51,712

Page 12
1. 54; 2. 5; 3. 9; 4. 24; 5. 4; 6. 6; 7. 30; 8. 6; 9. 12; 10. 48; 11. 63; 12. 10; 13. 7; 14. 12; 15. 12; 16. 12; 17. 7; 18. 7; 19. 8; 20. 2; 21. 5; 22. 3; 23. 5; 24. 9; 25. 4; 26. 8; 27. 9; 28. 11; 29. 4; 30. 5; 31. 4; 32. 8

Page 13
1. 530; 2. 240; 3. 1,290; 4. 1,040; 5. 2,100; 6. 500; 7. 780; 8. 480; 9. 350; 10. 1,080; 11. 1,760; 12. 1,150; 13. 18,750; 14. 12,720; 15. 3,880; 16. 8,640

Page 14
1. 1,740; 2. 102; 3. 460; 4. 1,542; 5. 2,190; 6. 612; 7. 6,160; 8. 2,898; 9. 756; 10. 2,535; 11. 1,488; 12. 58,311; 13. 4,459,092; 14. 5,468; 15. 6,741

Answer Key

Page 15
1. 3,567; 2. 1,566; 3. 720; 4. 2,070;
5. 1,562; 6. 7,310; 7. 901; 8. 3,589;
9. 1,274; 10. 2,584; 11. 1,625; 12. 432

Page 16
1. 10,833; 2. 10,720; 3. 8,928;
4. 18,262; 5. 5,180; 6. 23,760;
7. 7,956; 8. 13,962; 9. 9,243;
10. 25,376; 11. 18,391; 12. 21,009;
13. 29,700; 14. 13,110; 15. 17,346

Page 17
1. 19; 2. 26; 3. 42; 4. 93; 5. 49; 6. 28;
7. 84; 8. 67; 9. 65

Page 18
1. 17 R1; 2. 33 R1; 3. 1 R6; 4. 11 R2;
5. 14 R1; 6. 8 R3; 7. 155 R2; 8. 119 R1;
9. 229 R2

Page 19
1. 12 R63; 2. 14 R25; 3. 96 R8;
4. 4 R13; 5. 2 R34; 6. 28 R8; 7. 13 R13;
8. 12 R57; 9. 12 R40

Page 20
1. 52 R1; 2. 92 R92; 3. 46 R40;
4. 83 R9; 5. 69 R11; 6. 91 R59;
7. 79 R16; 8. 55 R26

Page 21
1. 5,728; 2. 2,128; 3. 124; 4. 464

Page 22
1. 3×7; 2. 3×5; 3. 5×11; 4. $2 \times 2 \times 2 \times 2$; 5. $2 \times 5 \times 5$; 6. $3 \times 3 \times 2$;
7. $5 \times 2 \times 2 \times 2$; 8. $2 \times 2 \times 2 \times 2 \times 2$;
9. $2 \times 2 \times 2 \times 3$

Page 23
1. $\frac{14}{20}, \frac{21}{30}$; 2. $\frac{6}{16}, \frac{9}{24}$; 3. $\frac{2}{4}, \frac{4}{8}, \frac{10}{20}$; 4. $\frac{4}{6}, \frac{6}{9}$;
5. $\frac{4}{10}, \frac{6}{15}, \frac{8}{20}$; 6. $\frac{2}{16}, \frac{3}{24}, \frac{4}{32}$; 7. $\frac{2}{8}, \frac{3}{12}$;
8. $\frac{2}{12}, \frac{3}{18}$

Page 24
1. 45; 2. 44; 3. 1; 4. 8; 5. 4; 6. 36; 7. 9;
8. 6; 9. 5; 10. 48; 11. 2; 12. 7

Page 25
1. $\frac{1}{2}$; 2. $\frac{2}{5}$; 3. $\frac{1}{3}$; 4. $\frac{2}{3}$; 5. $\frac{1}{3}$; 6. $\frac{3}{5}$;
7. $\frac{3}{4}$; 8. $\frac{1}{12}$; 9. $\frac{2}{3}$; 10. $\frac{1}{3}$; 11. $\frac{1}{4}$; 12. $\frac{5}{6}$

Page 26
1. $4\frac{2}{3}$; 2. $3\frac{1}{5}$; 3. $2\frac{3}{5}$; 4. $1\frac{1}{8}$; 5. $1\frac{5}{8}$;
6. $3\frac{1}{2}$; 7. $6\frac{1}{3}$; 8. $1\frac{2}{5}$; 9. $2\frac{1}{2}$; 10. $2\frac{1}{5}$;
11. $1\frac{1}{7}$; 12. $2\frac{2}{5}$; 13. $2\frac{1}{7}$; 14. $1\frac{2}{17}$;
15. $2\frac{1}{8}$

Page 27
1. $\frac{14}{3}$; 2. $\frac{19}{4}$; 3. $\frac{16}{5}$; 4. $\frac{10}{3}$; 5. $\frac{19}{3}$; 6. $\frac{13}{2}$;
7. $\frac{7}{4}$; 8. $\frac{13}{8}$; 9. $\frac{23}{8}$; 10. $\frac{11}{3}$; 11. $\frac{3}{2}$; 12. $\frac{29}{6}$;
13. $\frac{26}{5}$; 14. $\frac{23}{16}$

Page 28
1. LCD = 15; 2. LCD = 6;
3. LCD = 10; 4. LCD = 20;
5. LCD = 21; 6. LCD = 33;
7. LCD = 10; 8. LCD = 14;
9. LCD = 24

Page 29
1. $\frac{4}{5}$; 2. $\frac{2}{3}$; 3. $\frac{2}{3}$; 4. $\frac{1}{3}$; 5. $\frac{3}{7}$; 6. $\frac{1}{2}$;
7. $\frac{5}{12}$; 8. $\frac{7}{10}$; 9. $\frac{5}{6}$; 10. $\frac{4}{11}$; 11. $\frac{3}{4}$; 12. $\frac{7}{9}$

Page 30
1. $\frac{1}{4}$; 2. $\frac{1}{6}$; 3. $\frac{2}{3}$; 4. $\frac{3}{7}$; 5. $\frac{5}{6}$; 6. $\frac{3}{5}$;
7. $\frac{2}{5}$; 8. $\frac{1}{3}$; 9. $\frac{1}{2}$

Page 31
1. $\frac{17}{24}$; 2. $\frac{5}{6}$; 3. $1\frac{7}{20}$; 4. $\frac{23}{24}$; 5. $1\frac{1}{12}$; 6. $1\frac{11}{30}$

Page 32
1. $\frac{1}{20}$; 2. $\frac{11}{18}$; 3. $\frac{1}{8}$; 4. $\frac{4}{9}$; 5. $\frac{1}{3}$; 6. $\frac{1}{5}$

Page 33
1. $7\frac{1}{6}$; 2. $5\frac{11}{12}$; 3. $8\frac{1}{4}$; 4. $7\frac{11}{15}$; 5. $6\frac{11}{12}$;
6. $4\frac{1}{24}$

Page 34
1. $1\frac{5}{7}$; 2. $2\frac{2}{3}$; 3. $\frac{1}{3}$; 4. $5\frac{3}{4}$; 5. $2\frac{3}{5}$;
6. $\frac{3}{5}$

Answer Key

Page 35
1. $1\frac{7}{24}$; 2. $1\frac{11}{12}$; 3. $1\frac{7}{12}$; 4. $5\frac{13}{21}$

Page 36
1. $\frac{1}{4}$; 2. $\frac{2}{5}$; 3. $\frac{2}{7}$; 4. $\frac{5}{9}$; 5. $\frac{1}{10}$; 6. $\frac{1}{3}$;
7. $\frac{1}{16}$; 8. $\frac{4}{7}$; 9. $\frac{1}{12}$

Page 37
1. 2; 2. $1\frac{3}{5}$; 3. $\frac{6}{7}$; 4. $1\frac{1}{7}$; 5. $2\frac{2}{5}$; 6. $\frac{9}{10}$;
7. $6\frac{3}{4}$; 8. $1\frac{4}{5}$; 9. $1\frac{1}{3}$

Page 38
1. $\frac{9}{16}$; 2. $\frac{7}{9}$; 3. $1\frac{1}{2}$; 4. $1\frac{1}{7}$; 5. $\frac{7}{8}$; 6. $2\frac{1}{10}$;
7. $1\frac{1}{3}$; 8. $3\frac{1}{2}$; 9. $1\frac{7}{12}$

Page 39
0.006; 0.036; 0.10; 0.027; 0.92; 0.047;
0.89; 0.2; 0.08

Page 40
1. 3.6; 2. 6.01; 3. 1.08; 4. 7.2; 5. 3.032;
6. 4.002; 7. 108.7; 8. 64.02; 9. 82.05;
10. 81.5; 11. 42.093; 12. 11.27

Page 41
1. 5.7; 2. 7.4; 3. 5.4; 4. 8.6; 5. 33.0;
6. 7.4; 7. 69; 8. 5; 9. 26.6; 10. 122.2;
11. 80.8; 12. 3.05; 13. 9.92; 14. 8.04;
15. 62.69; 16. 4.77; 17. 27.98; 18. 1.59;
19. 5.82; 20. 3.25; 21. 51.97; 22. 81.75;
23. 6.38

Page 42
1. <; 2. <; 3. >; 4. >; 5. >; 6. >; 7. <;
8. <; 9. =; 10. <; 11. >; 12. =; 13. <;
14. <

Page 43
$1.05, $1.07, $1.10, $1.25, $2.03,
$2.15, $2.21, $2.51; 1. 4.50; 2. 10.57;
3. 2.52; 4. 1.847; 5. 89.90

Page 44
1. 71.12; 2. 101.09; 3. 190.82; 4. 21.43;
5. 188.25; 6. 397.8; 7. 171.71; Cheetah

Page 45
1. 950.12; 2. 18.34; 3. 1,079.15;
4. 139.83; 5. 150.967; 6. 323.12;
7. 90.62; 8. 1,156.42; 9. 0.219;
Dragonfly

Page 46
1. 23.76; 2. 45.36; 3. 219.3;
4. 1,316.88; 5. 210.924; 6. 279.45;
7. 582.684; 8. 39.216; 9. 22.4536

Page 47
1. 0.28; 2. 0.324; 3. 15.66; 4. 50.4;
5. 0.0084; 6. 0.4344; 7. 0.4002;
8. 3,233.925; 9. 4,413.465

Page 48
1. 4.25; 2. 0.57; 3. 27.9; 4. 12.28;
5. 0.245; 6. 7.98; 7. 0.76; 8. 0.913;
9. 0.614

Page 49
1. 89; 2. 23.6; 3. 45.9; 4. 78.8; 5. 69.1;
6. 38.6

Page 50
1. 9%; 2. 4%; 3. 30%; 4. 50%; 5. 80%;
6. 10%; 7. $\frac{50}{100}$, $\frac{33}{100}$, $\frac{65}{100}$, $\frac{56}{100}$, $\frac{30}{100}$, $\frac{5}{100}$; 8. $\frac{1}{2}$, $\frac{33}{100}$,
$\frac{13}{20}$, $\frac{14}{25}$, $\frac{3}{10}$, $\frac{1}{20}$

Page 51
1. $\frac{14}{100}$, 0.14; 2. 0.27, 27%; 3. $\frac{32}{100}$, 0.32;
4. $\frac{89}{100}$, 89%; 5. $\frac{57}{100}$, 0.57; 6. $\frac{17}{100}$, 17%;
7. 0.71, 71%; 8. $\frac{43}{100}$, 0.43; 9. $\frac{34}{100}$, 34%;
10. 0.64, 64%; 11. $\frac{75}{100}$, 75%

Page 52
1. <; 2. >; 3. <; 4. >; 5. >; 6. >; 7. =;
8. >; 9. >; 10. <; 11. <; 12. <

Answer Key

Page 53
1. 1; 2. 1; 3. -11; 4. 9; 5. -9; 6. -1; 7. 3;
8. -2; 9. 14; 10. 5; 11. 1; 12. -7; 13. B, 2

Page 54
1. a = 10; 2. c = 6; 3. e = 20;
4. g = 3.6; 5. i = 11.8; 6. k = 15;
7. m = 68; 8. b = 13; 9. d = 4;
10. f = 11; 11. h = 5; 12. j = 2.9

Page 55

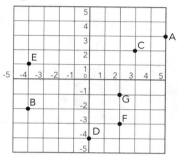

1. (-1,-2); 2. (2,-2); 3. (3,2); 4. (1,1);
5. (-2,-1); 6. (-3,2)

Page 56
1. (2,2); 2. (2,-1); 3. (-2,-2); 4. (-4,3);
5. (4,1); 6. (3,-3)

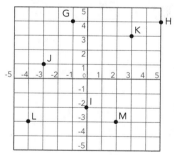

Page 57
1. 3 ft.; 2. 8 in.; 3. 7 yd.; 4. 5 ft.;
5. 60 in.; 6. 14 ft.; 7. 10,560 in.;
8. 87 in.; 9. 16,150 ft.; 10. 158 in.;
11. 69 ft.

Page 58
1. m; 2. m; 3. cm; 4. 4,200 cm;
5. 4,000 m; 6. 850 mm; 7. 3 m;
8. 80 cm; 9. 2 km

Page 59
1. 48 m; 2. 35 m; 3. 36 in.; 4. 74 cm;
5. 24 in.; 6. 106 ft.

Page 60
1. 63 in.^{2}; 2. 55 ft.^{2}; 3. 48 m^2;
4. 24 cm^2; 5. 77 m^2; 6. 25 in.^{2}

Page 61
1. 378 ft.^{2}; 2. 1,632 in.^{2}; 3. 200 ft.;
4. 1,036 in.

Page 62
1. 216 m^3; 2. 160 in.^{3}; 3. 41.35 m^3;
4. 240 mm^3; 5. no, 360 ft.^{3}

Page 63
1. line; 2. ray; 3. line segment;
4. intersecting; 5. parallel;
6. intersecting; 7. perpendicular

Page 64
1. acute; 2. right; 3. right; 4. obtuse;
5. obtuse; 6. acute; 7. obtuse;
8. acute

Page 65
1. congruent; 2. congruent;
3. similar; 4. similar

Page 66
1. mean: 16, median: 10, mode: 10,
range: 27; 2. mean: 15, median: 14,
mode: 14, range: 22

Page 67
1. April; 2. January; 3. 0.5 inches;
4. 0.875 inches

Page 68
1. Figure skating; 2. 16%;
3. Snowboarding; 4. 21%; 5. 34%

Answer Key

Page 69
1. March; 2. February and May;
3. 120; 4. increased by 40;
5. 160 TVs; 6. 120

Page 70
1. 8642; 2. 8647; 3. 8644; 4. 8643;
5. 6643; 6. 6543; 7. 4543

Page 71
1. $k \div 5$; 2. $v + 5$; 3. $y - 7$; 4. $6 \times s$, $6s$,
or $6(s)$; 5. $12 \div j$; 6. $15 - t$; 7. $c + 20$;
8. twelve times e; 9. w plus 34;
10. thirty-six divided by m;
11. q minus 6; 12. n minus 3;
13. seven times z

Page 72
(Top row): B, D; (Second row): A, B;
(Third row): D, A; (Last row): C, C

Page 73
Answers will vary but may include:
1. The shortest route is 21 miles.

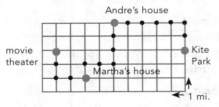

Mark's tree fort
Evan's house
Skate Park
← 1.5 mi.

2. The distance is 17 miles.

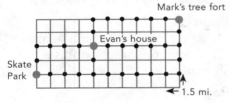

Andre's house
movie theater
Martha's house
Kite Park
← 1 mi.

Page 74
1. 9; 2. 6; 3. 12, 6; 4. 9, 12, 15;
5.

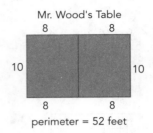

Mr. Wood's Table
8   8
10   10
8   8
perimeter = 52 feet

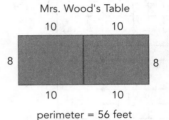

Mrs. Wood's Table
10   10
8   8
10   10
perimeter = 56 feet

Page 75

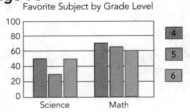

Favorite Subject by Grade Level
Science   Math
4
5
6

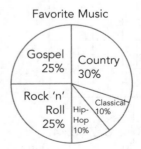

Favorite Music
Gospel 25%
Country 30%
Rock 'n' Roll 25%
Hip-Hop 10%
Classical 10%